Contents

Introduction

This is the story of how my family's religious beliefs have created psychological disorders in their children. Everything from exorcisms to supposed demon possessions went on in my household.

These experiences caused me to develop phobias that are at times life altering. My autistic sister did not respond very positively to any of her exorcisms or prayer circles, as anyone familiar with autism could imagine.

My sister Jenny is an autistic adult in her 20s now, and while she can't tell me about her childhood experiences, she must have had a scary first few years. Before and just after she was diagnosed, my mother would drag her into prayer circles or have exorcisms performed on her.

Autistic people as a general rule cannot handle being overstimulated. I generally avoided these rituals, whether they took place on impulse at a tent revival by a strip mall or in our living room on a Friday night. I am sure that her intentions were good, but the results of her actions are more important than her intent.

"This is the only way to help her."

"But she's scared."

"It's the evil spirit that is scared!"

The thing that bothers me the most is how superstition and lack of knowledge caused me to live in absolute terror every time I went to sleep from about the ages of 13 to 17. I suffered from what is known as sleep paralysis. The short explanation is that your brain wakes up in stages and mine were out of sync during those years.

The cognitive side of my brain would wake up before the side responsible for motor skills. This meant that I would wake up, be able to see what was going on around me, but was unable to move. It is a very uncomfortable and frightful experience that can be accompanied by hallucinations.

Like any child, I went to my parents for help.

Their explanation was that a spirit of some kind, probably a dead relative, was trying to possess me. I don't know anyone that could come out of that trauma free.

"Mommy, when I wake up from a nightmare, I can't move my body and I feel tingly like I've been sleeping on my arm. I tell my toes to move and try so hard, but it doesn't work. I wake up exhausted and scared. What's wrong with me?"

"It's a spirit trying to take your body. We'll put a clear glass of water in the highest place in the room to filter them out. Your grandfather also just died, he may be the one doing it."

I should explain the religious ideologies of my parents before I go into any of these stories any further. My father was a complicated man who struck me as an agnostic who was spiritual based on his own experiences.

My mother was always Christian, but with an odd and unorthodox spiritualism that doesn't quite fit into the Christian mold. I would describe her as being a severely superstitious woman who fancies herself a clairvoyant with a gift for premonitions.

She claims to have seen the future on many different occasions, but it has always 'changed' or altered itself in some way when it happened differently than she was 'told' it would be. There were many winning lottery tickets, 'true loves' and accidents that didn't happen because 'plans change.'

As an adult, I humor her and don't take her seriously. As a child and young lady, I wanted to believe everything that my mother said. I would furiously daydream or change all of my plans based on some good or bad vision or feeling she would say that she had.

If my car broke down or I got sick, it was always a sign that I should cancel my vacation or not do something that I had been planning.

"You were wrong about him mom, very wrong. He couldn't have ever been my true love. He just told his family he's gay."

"Plans changed, sweetie. The future is always changing. I only saw one of the futures. You should have just waited for him to come around."

My father was scientifically minded, but had an experience with Santeria in Cuba that changed his mind and pushed him into something that he did not talk about. My mother spoke of him performing astral projections, having a spirit guide and a secret name.

There was also a shell necklace that was always hidden from me. Every time I came close to touching it, I would get yelled at as if I were about to touch a venomous snake. The spiritual landscape of my childhood was quite varied and confusing to say the least.

These unseen, spiritual parts of my world were explained to me as a child as being as real as the world that I saw. That meant that all of the good things, as well as the bad, were real.

Superstitious Spiritual Cleansings

Big Tent Revival Prayer Circle

Exorcism Events

"Whatever is wrong with her must be
pulled out by the horns!"

She was about three years old when everyone agreed that something was definitely wrong with her development. She stopped making eye contact, stopped talking and was very violent. She got everything that she wanted so long as it would keep her quiet and happy for any amount of time.

It was probably the violence and outrageous behavior that drove my mother to believe that it had to be some spirit doing all of this and not her adorable, blue-eyed daughter. No doctor seemed to be able to pinpoint her condition. She went undiagnosed until she was eight years old.

Until then, she would go into rages and bite my mother hard enough to draw blood. She resisted potty training and would go just about anywhere that she wanted. She would go into wild fits when we went out if she could not take everything she wanted home with her.

She even had a thing for throwing all of the folded clothes out of every drawer in the house and peeing on them. She must have been very, very mad about something.

My mom decided that what was wrong was spiritual and not mental. She began trying to take her into church. The church we went to was Catholic, and the imagery inside was intense.

Everything from huge, suffering Christ sculptures to burning candles must have set my sister off. She acted like she was very much in the last place that she wanted to be. My mother took this as a sign.

"Why is she acting that way as soon as she walks in the church?"

"It must be that something in her cannot stand to be here. We need a spiritual intervention!"

I am only two years older than my sister, so it obviously scared me to death that something might be inside of her. I was afraid of her until I realized that my mother had to be wrong.

Big Tent Revival

We all went out as a family to Woolworth to buy clothes in the bad part of town one day when I was 7 and Jenny was 5. It was dark when we came out of the store. My mother noticed a giant, white tent on one end of the parking lot full of people dancing, singing and praising God.

They were so loud that we could hear them from almost a city block away.

She decided that this was a sign and that she needed to take my sister to them. My dad was horribly against it. He said that there was no way of knowing what kind of people they were or if the stimulation would be bad for Jenny.

My mother had her way and dragged my sister out into the giant tent of praying strangers.

"This is a sign! She can be healed today! I feel it!"

"Those people are just going to take advantage of your situation."

"She will be healed tonight!"

My father and I both sat in the car while he brooded. He was very much against what was about to happen. I got very bored after a while and decided to go make sure that she didn't make us wait in the parking lot all night.

It was bright in the tent, everyone was wearing light colors and the music seemed to be writhing in tempo with the people. There were people laying hands on my sister, praying with all of their might.

It was a circle of happy believers that thought anything was possible. I could tell by the look on their faces that they really thought that if they held onto Jenny long enough and prayed hard and long enough, that she would walk out of there talking and acting like a normal girl.

While I could tell that they were good people and I liked them, I did not like the look on my sister's face while a strange, obese, dark-skinned woman laid a hand on her forehead and babbled in a string of incoherent sounds.

Jenny looked terrified. There were dozens of hands touching her, reaching out to her with sweaty palms. Jenny's eyes were wide and she looked like she was in the worst situation that she could've imagined.

She didn't like to be touched and she hated loud sounds. The torment she was in was plain even to me at such a young age. She looked overwhelmed and bullied.

I had seen my cat swat mice around before and Jenny had the same expression on her face that that poor mouse had. It was a look of being in a world that was out of your control and knowing that the worst may yet be coming.

My mother held her down and made her take the prayers, desperately hoping that this would all work. Meanwhile, the main woman was yelling louder and louder towards the heavens and in my sister's face. Jenny was the center of all of the loud, unwanted attention.

She would only have been in greater torment if she had actually been in hell.

I let someone in the circle pray for me and then made my way over to my mother. I rained on her parade and told her that we had to get back. I may have even had to tell her someone was feeling sick in order to get her out of there.

We all piled into the car and drove home, my sister worse for wear.

Exorcism Prayer Circle

The most vivid of prayer events that I remember my mother putting my sister through happened on a Friday night when I was around 10 years old. I can still remember being irritated when a large group of strange women came over when all I wanted to do was watch Family Matters, The Simpsons and Are You Afraid of the Dark.

The mood was very serious and they were talking in the low tones adults use when something is very wrong. My father had the good sense to set me up in another room with a TV while they were getting started with whatever it was that they planned to do.

I was barely 10 minutes into The Simpsons when I heard chanting and humming of scary-movie proportions coming from down the hall.

It doesn't take much to make an impression on someone so young. What I saw would have made an impression on just about anyone. The living room was dark except for warm, amber light shining off of candles.

Every woman had linked their arms, creating an impassible human circle and praying and chanting with my sister in the center. An older woman that often babysat us was leading the group, grabbing Jenny's head and telling the devil to get out of her in a voice that scared me.

Jenny was terrified. Her eyes were wide and I could tell that everything in her being wanted to run. Everyone was slowly swaying side to side, their heads down and eyes closed while they prayed.

They were yelling at something that they thought was inside of Jenny to get out of her, something was wrong with her and it, whatever it was, was at fault.

They shouted commands at Jenny's face, pushing their hands against her and leaving brief marks in her skin from the derisive force they were applying against this demon within her.

The problem was as easy as the solution to the people in that room with Jenny that night. They thought that all major problems were the fault of evil beings, and the only way to fix these problems was to cast the demons out.

I only hope that Jenny did not understand what they were saying, because it would have been much more traumatizing to have been convinced that something innately evil inhabited her body than to have just had a terrible night.

I asked what was going on and told someone (I can't remember who) that they were just upsetting her, but I was sent off so that they could continue their work. I peeked in many times throughout the evening to see what was happening.

In my mind, one of two things could happen: Jenny could go into a biting rage or she could miraculously come out of her autism and ask for a cheeseburger. Neither happened, but Jenny was inconsolable and excitable for a while.

My Sleep Paralysis

Demonic Terror

Alone and Forgotten

Finding the Truth

"If you can't control what is happening to your body, then it is a demon trying to possess you."

Demonic Terror

One morning when I was barely 13, I woke up and couldn't stretch my legs. I tried as hard as I could, but nothing budged. I tried to move my arms and the same non-event occurred. I wondered if I was dreaming, but I could see my surroundings and knew that I was awake.

I couldn't lift my head off the pillow or even turn over on my back. My body felt tingly, as if a million little needs were stinging me. There was also a pressure on my chest, as if something was pushing on it.

After what felt like an eternity in hell, my toes finally responded to my constant pushing against my body and moved. I felt more exhausted than I had before I went to bed. The experience took everything out of me.

I spent every moment that I was paralyzed fighting it and panicking in my mind. While I can't remember if I went to my mother right away or after a few more nights just like this, I remember what she said. At first, she was rational about it. She suggested that maybe I had fallen asleep on my arm and I had a general lack of blood flow.

We couldn't afford pillows a few years before, so I had made it a habit to fall asleep cradling my own head. When I started actually using a pillow and nothing improved, she began to seriously consider that it was an evil spirit. Imagine being a month past your 12th birthday and thinking that an evil spirit is trying to possess you every morning.

It is not a mentally healthy way to start your teenage years.

My mother started off by placing a clear glass of water in the highest place in the room. She said that any spirits entering the room would get filtered through it and be unable to get to me. At some point she brought the bible into my room and had me sleep next to it.

When that did not make a difference either, the bible went under my pillow. A Christian cross necklace even came into play. I prayed every night of course, like any reasonable 13 year old who was told by an authority figure that her sleep paralysis was an evil spirit trying to take her body.

I remember overhearing a conversation between my parents about the recent death of my paternal grandfather. He was a rather unsavory character that my father had not been on speaking terms with since his early adulthood.

My father made himself clear – he thought this 'spirit' was my grandfather trying to take my body in order to make me successful so that he could make up for his bad parenting.

Alone and Forgotten

Over time, my sleep paralysis just became a nonissue with my parents, since nothing they did could fix it. Not prayers, not glasses of water, not holy scripture at my bedside. It just kept happening until it eventually happened less and less.

Even when I was 15 and the Internet was available to me, I didn't think to research what was happening to me. I just sort of accepted my waking terror as a part of my life. I still thought that the pressure on my chest was indelible proof that it was indeed a spirit (thanks, mom!), but I figured that the fact that I kept coming out of it meant that someone upstairs was on my side.

I even went as far as to call a prayer hotline one night after I accidentally dozed off and couldn't move for a few minutes after waking up. The poor girl on the other end was audibly shaken by my saying, 'A demon just tried to possess my body.'

I became very religious for a few of my teen years, all the time wondering why my faith was not protecting me from the things that were making a good night's sleep completely impossible for me. I still fight sleep out of pure habit to this day. Even my religious uncle would chide me for not 'believing enough' to keep colds at bay.

If I could not believe truly enough to pray away a cold, then what could I do about a spirit trying to seize my body? While I never told my uncle about my paralysis, I did ask him about muscle spasms that would sometimes happen when I was falling asleep.

Laughing at me, he said, "Anything moving your body that is not you is the enemy (a demon)."

Even involuntary muscle spasms while falling asleep were a definite sign of a demon to him. I didn't dare tell him about the all-out paralysis that I experienced when I'd wake up.

It didn't seem to matter what I did or how hard I tried to be a spiritually strong person. It did not help any muscle spasms or sleeping problems. What other conclusion is a young girl to come to other than she is doomed in some way?

Learning the Truth

My sleep paralysis happened much less in my late teens and a only handful of times in my 20s. It was in my developmental psychology class in college that I read about sleep paralysis. Nothing I can say could ever really do justice to the relief that I felt rush through me.

Everything that I had been going through could be explained medically. There were no evil beings out to get me. There had not been any painful, exhausting struggles for my soul all of those mornings and nights. My brain was waking up out of sync with itself for a few years.

I was relieved, but I was also angry. I spent every night for several years so scared of sleep that I did it as little as possible. I woke up from every catnap thinking that some dark, unseen creature was trying to take my consciousness out of the equation.

I fought and pushed and inwardly screamed every single day for years because my mother and father had confirmed that whatever was happening was spiritual, and it was evil. Something specifically wanted me and no one else that I knew. That caused me to doubt what kind of person I was underneath of the goodness that I always strived to achieve.

Their superstitions, gross lack of knowledge and failure to look for logical answers for their suffering daughter made the already unpleasant experience that sleep paralysis is into something a whole lot worse. Instead of being a normal kid, I distanced myself from my peers because of what I thought was fundamentally different about our worlds.

Who can think of making friends, playing with other kids at recess or sitting with other kids during lunch when they're exhausted from fighting demons off every morning? I lost those important developmental opportunities to socially interact with my peers and create connections with other human beings. As an adult, I am still paying for those years lived in fear.

My Father's Undiagnosed Bipolar Disorder

Childhood Rages

My Mother Blaming Me

Later Changes in Character

"I'm not sure that you're right about that."

"I'm not wrong. Are you saying I'm stupid? Are you saying that I should as well be dead, I'm so stupid? Here, let me cut my veins. Take the knife. Here are my veins just for you. Cut them! I'm so stupid you should cut them for me!"

Childhood Rages

Everything about my world and my family was beautiful and happy until Jenny started exhibiting developmental problems.

We all went out as a family, had vacations and always had dinners together at the kitchen table. My father was a generally well-natured man who gave me gifts every Friday and fed me straight from his dinner plate whenever I decided that his food looked much better than mine.

It was a happy world of family connections and Saturday morning cartoons. There was no better time of the day than when my father came home from work for his hugs. Those were my favorite times.

When no one knew what was wrong with Jenny or how to fix her oppositional behavior, my father's rages started. My mother would be busy picking up after Jenny's messes and not get a chance to start dinner until just before my father was due back from work.

She would spend the day picking up Jenny's feces (she refused to be potty trained until she was 8), picking up all of the broken notebook paper Jenny would litter around the house, scrubbing crayon and marker doodles off of walls and re-washing clean clothes that Jenny had just made piles of and urinated on.

With that in mind, picture my father coming home after a grueling 12 hour workday at an industrial mechanic's shop. She would either have just been able to start dinner or had it heating up.

He would come barreling into the trailer with a sour look on his face, ready to tear apart anything in his path. He'd hear that he had to wait for dinner and it would all begin.

"I work all day and you can't even have my food ready when I come home?! Am I not important enough to get dinner ready in time for? Am I some worthless dog off of the street?"

Punch! There would go a part of a wall.

"Why do I even buy food for if I can't eat it?!"

He would lunge forward and open the refrigerator doors, throwing food on the floor as violently as he could. Not satisfied that this was destructive enough, he would grab the refrigerator on both sides and threw it halfway across the kitchen, food splattering everywhere while my mother begged and screamed while I watched from my door.

This was a regular spectacle. Instead of running to my daddy when he came home, I would be locked in the bedroom with my sister. I'd watch what was happening from a hole that my father put in that door at some point.

Only bodies were off limits when he was angry. He sought to manipulate and destroy you emotionally, not physically. If he was upset that the electric bill was too high, he would go into a rage and tear the air conditioning window unit right out of the wall and slam it into the floor, damaging the tiles underneath.

If he was angry that I was not doing something that he wanted me to do, like get off of the phone, he would take a kitchen knife and threaten to cut his veins if I didn't do what he wanted.

"You are treating me like I don't matter. I might as well not live, here; I'm going to cut my veins. You want me to die; you want me to cut my veins. Here, I'll do it for you."

All the while he would expose his veins and hold the knife directly to them. He would kill himself and it would be on me.

He finally took the knife and cut the phone cord so that I could not keep talking on it. Now there was no phone for anyone and everyone could blame me for it. He made it clear to everyone who was within listening distance; we no longer had a working phone and it was all my fault.

My Mother Blaming Me

I remember my father walking away from the refrigerator he had thrown on the floor, its contents broken and everywhere. He left my crying mother to get on her hands and knees and try to clean it all up.

She pointed at me and said, "This is all your fault. I would have had dinner ready if you had just watched your sister."

I would like to point out that I was 5 and my incredibly violent sister was 3. I would argue the point with her.

"It's not my fault that this happened."

"Yes it is. I'm locking you up with your sister from now on."

And so I was. I was given full responsibility over her and locked into a room with nothing but bathroom privileges the entire day for many years. The windows even had chicken wire bolted over them from the outside so that we could not get out. I would sit at the window and stare out the 1/4 inch openings for hours, watching the birds and wishing that I could fly with them.

That was when I promised myself that I would see the world one day. It took many years for me to keep from panicking whenever a room that I was in was locked. Anything from a trip to a fast food restaurant to playing in the yard was a wonderful adventure in the world at that point in my life.

My father still raged out when dinner wasn't right on time with his arrival. Even with me locked away with Jenny, dinner was too late or too cold for him.

At one point when I was about 8, my father looked me in the eyes and cruelly said, "Goodbye honey, see you on the weekends."

After he walked out the door, my mother looked at me with tears in her eyes and said, "This is all your fault! He's leaving because you weren't watching Jenny."

I had enough sense from watching after-school specials about divorced families to know that this was not my fault. I argued as much too. "This isn't my fault. It's between you and dad."

It didn't matter what I had to say, my mother thought then, as she still does now, that his leaving that day was my fault. They worked out whatever the argument was about a few weeks later, but the damage they both did by targeting me could not be undone.

Later Changes of Character

It is safe to say that my father's rages mellowed out as time went on. It changed from constant explosions to a disturbing change in character that was often accompanied by verbally abusive or manipulative banter.

On a trip home from the beach one day, everyone was glowing from having such a great time. Our swimsuits were drying, the sand was still between our toes and we smelled of ocean and barbecue. He was having a conversation with my mother that went very wrong for some reason and decided to tell everyone in the car that he was too stupid to drive.

"I'm stupid, everyone! I'm so stupid that I don't know the gas from the brake!" He'd slam the brake.

We'd all yell in fear and beg him to stop.

"Are you all saying I'm not driving right? I'm too stupid to drive?!" He'd slam the brake in moving traffic again and get out of the car, stomping his way to the sidewalk and acting like he was going to walk home.

We would all beg him to stop and come back of course, our hearts in our throats. He'd eventually come back, we'd stop for fast food on the way home and pretend it never happened. All the while, a large knot of anxiety had formed in my chest and would not leave.

Even a happy dinner at the table could not be happy for very long with him. When I was a teenager, we all moved into a nice house and things were looking up. My mother made dinner and we were all sitting at the new wooden table.

My chest had that knot in it again. I was so scared that I would lose the happy moment that we were having at any time. I had good reason to think that.

My father decided that the food was too bland for his taste. My new brother, Edwin, was also autistic and tried to help. He poured salt on my father's plate, but the shaker top fell off and the entire container emptied out.

My father was about to explode, he had already slammed his hands with tremendous force against the sides of the table and had that horrible expression on his face. Something in me burst and I impulsively flipped his plate facedown and ran to my bedroom.

He yelled behind me, throwing potted plants at me as I ran. I narrowly missed being hit by two. One broke right by the heel of my foot. I locked the door behind me and got in the fetal position with my back against the door.

He began to roughly knock on the door with his fists. When I wouldn't let him in, he began to throw his entire body against it. He would have barged in and broken right through if it weren't for me pushing against the door with my legs propped up against a piece of furniture.

Even in his final days, when he was well aware that he had been a monster in the past, he was not immune to character faults. He often looked at me lovingly and apologized for how he behaved, saying that he had no idea how I came out as well as I did.

These statements usually followed him telling me that I was worthless, a complete failure of a daughter and someone that any man would want to leave. I slaved away for him when he was sick, running his errands and doing everything that the household needed in order to function.

Being told that I was a 'good for nothing' and that he understood 'why my ex left me' after spending 7 hours buying driveway sealant two towns over and actually sealing the driveway because I didn't have time to go to the post office before catching a movie has a way of starting breakdowns. I snapped that day, the subject of my ex being a very sore one. I destroyed all of the nice things that I worked so hard to buy and stopped short of hurting myself.

It is never OK to hurt yourself, but if anyone ever drove me close to it, it was my father. He had a way of saying the most painful thing possible that would get deep down into your soul and decimate it.

Bullying

Public School

Private School

"Shut up. I can beat the sh*t out of you all I want and ain't no one gonna believe you over me."

Public School

My family was having a very rough time when I was in the first grade. I was withdrawn from the private school I was attending without having it explained to me ahead of time and was enrolled in a public school by our trailer.

The neighborhood used to be largely uninhabited most of the year. Many European vacationers and snowbirds owned trailers in our park and stayed a few weeks or months out of the year. Everything was clean and well-manicured.

However, the park owner retired and the new owner had less stringent rules about applicants. It did not take long for the neighborhood to become extremely dangerous. Gang members moved in next door to us and stole all of my comic books and our cable boxes on one occasion.

Wearing a bandana of any kind was a death wish and I was scared to wear red or white. The world was safe in my private school on the other side of town. My new public school was in the hotbed inner-city violence.

The public school I now went to was hard on me for a lot of reasons. I didn't get to say goodbye to my friends in the private school and missed them terribly. In the new school, I instantly had something going against me: my light skin color.

There was a little boy at my table that had a crush on me in the 1st grade. He begged me to kiss him just about every single day. I didn't like him and always turned him down. One day, our teacher asked me why I didn't just kiss him.

Being a kid, I thought that you only kissed men you would marry and I had a particular taste in boys. I told her,

"I won't kiss him because I want to marry a tall blonde boy with blue eyes." My teacher's head just about exploded.

I was then subject to a lengthy lecture about how I was not white and that I had to kiss this boy. She forced me to kiss him and I felt awful about it afterwards. I told my mother about it and was withdrawn immediately.

It was only back in private school for another school year. They couldn't afford it and so I went back to another public school in the same area for the 3rd grade.

Here I could not even sit and have breakfast.

A friend and I got breakfast in the cafeteria and were ordered to sit apart and fill out the tables by school staff. I sat in a table full of girls that I didn't know who really hated my guts. They were harassing me the entire time I was just trying to eat.

"Go to your own white school. This is our school. You don't belong here. We don't want you." The four or five of them would not just let me eat.

I finished eating about the same time that my friend did and we both threw out our trays and walked outside of the building towards the basketball courts. The girls at breakfast followed me and grabbed me with my hands inside of my jacket pocket.

They threw me against a barbed-wire fence and all kicked and punched me at once, all the while yelling racial slurs on me. The thing I remember most was 'cracker.' I couldn't even begin to fight back.

My friend watched from a distance, looking rather helpless. No one helped of course, but a few people did gather around and yell, "A fight, a fight, a n***er and a white!"

My friend and I told our teacher what had happened and she made sure to have the girls called in and suspended. That suspension never happened. My mother decided that she would find out what was wrong in their lives and help them.

My mother wound up being very good friends with those girls. I never have forgiven her for letting them get away with treating me that way. Her intentions often made things at school much worse.

There was a boy in the fourth grade that wanted me dead. I don't mean that figuratively. I mean that he really wanted to kill me. We used to exchange banter at first, but it quickly escalated on his end. He didn't like whatever nickname it was that I made up for him and decided to bring knives to school and threaten to kill me and my mother.

My mother came to my school lunch for Thanksgiving celebrations and saw a fist fight break out a few tables over. She was horrified and went over there to break them up. They just kept slugging at each other, so she slammed the table and yelled at them to look at themselves.

This boy that wanted me dead was at this table. He decided to use this incident as an excuse and claimed that my mother hit his hand. I know this didn't happen, but it didn't really matter if it did. He started chasing me when school got out.

He and several of his friends would try to trip me so that they could beat me up right on the school lawn in front of my family. Every day was a life or death sprint to my mother's car. I even jumped over a foot meant to trip me several times.

This led to my becoming the school punching bag during P.E. I never cared much for the heat and would lean against cool concrete whenever we weren't being forced to do something. There was a slab of concrete that I would always lean against that was nearby where the line to leave P.E. would form.

This boy and all of his friends would line up and punch me in the back there. I'd tell them to stop, the teacher would see them doing it and tell them, "You boys better stop before she gets mad and hits you back."

But it kept on, 5 or more boys at a time. My mom brought me to the principal's office to see about getting me transferred or disciplining all of the people punching me and threatening to kill me.

Her response while sipping her diet soda was, "I can't do nothing about that.

You will just have to settle your differences with those girls."

"They are boy ma'am."

"Boys? Well, you'll just have to settle your differences. We don't do transfers for disagreements among students."

My mother handled that transfer herself. She took her life savings and put me in a private school.

Private School

Private school is a different monster than public school. At this point, I was the opposite of a well-adjusted kid. My family still lived in a trailer and these children were all from middle-income families with no real financial problems.

I no longer knew how to get along with someone else my age without assuming that they were out to get me in some way. Many of these kids treated me very differently once they found out where I lived.

I couldn't afford to get my hair cut in a hair salon then. My mother or father cut it at home and often messed it up. I couldn't afford the highlights that all of the other 5th grade girls had. I didn't wear nice gold jewelry like them either.

I didn't think that they were better than me or worth more. I just wished I could have those nice things too. I also thought that the ones that brushed me off because I was 'too poor' were snobs.

I had a great friend that I did everything with. I will call her Rosy for the purposes of this book. Rosy and I made up stories together and were the best of friends. That is, until her family came to visit me at home.

It wasn't long after her family saw our trailer that Rosy said she couldn't be friends with me anymore. She even told me that her parents said they were surprised that their car was still there when they left.

I wasn't the kind of person that she should be friends with. She cut me off, just like that. We were friends on and off later on in life, but that kind of rejection sticks with you.

I started to blossom into womanhood at this time. In the 6th grade

I was ready for my first bra. My mom was in some kind of funk or was depressed from spending all of her money on my private school, because I was largely neglected.

I had no deodorant and would often smell. My hair was often greasy and we had nothing for me to wash my hair with. We didn't have a brush at home and my hair was a mess. My school uniform didn't have a zipper sewn into the skirt (a manufacturing error) and she refused to replace it because "she was not made out of money" and "it was probably my fault and not the store's."

I not only had the worst hair, the most unsavory scent, and a dire need for a training bra, but I was also the only girl who had to pull her blouse over her skirt instead of tucking it in. This was not an easy transition at all.

A teacher that had never had me in a class pulled me into the bathroom one day and gave me a bag of things that I needed. It had shampoo, conditioner (which I had never heard of before), deodorant and a brush. I couldn't have been more excited if it had been Christmas.

I showed my mother my goodies that night and she was insulted.

"Who do they think you are, giving you charity?"

"Well, I did need it."

A girl that felt bad for me gave me one of her old bras. It was too small, but I was thrilled to wear it. My father finally said enough was enough and made my mother take me out to buy me a bra.

She had waited so long to take me to get one that I was actually a 36B when I finally got my own bra. That's a bra size that I kept well through my teenage years. I still don't understand why she refused to help me blend in with the other girls by getting me the things that I needed. It is a difficult age for any girl to transition into, never mind a girl that is the poorest of her peers.

Conclusion

If my parents had been sensible and sought out a doctor for me and accepted that Jenny's issues were purely chemical and not spiritual, we would have been much better off. I can't speculate about Jenny's life or how she sees the world.

What I can say is that their gross belief in superstition and medical ignorance made everything much worse than it already was to begin with.

It goes without saying that my mind has some long-term trauma to deal with. I now suffer from an anxiety disorder that kicks in whenever I think about evil spirits or demons. Even writing about it is difficult for me.

I have to take a pretty high dosage of antidepressants that doubles as an anti-anxiety medication to keep attacks at bay. An anxiety attack is a pretty bad experience. An internal fear tremble will involuntarily begin, my stomach will turn and I can end up in a full tremor.

My body temperature will drop to such an extent that my husband has actually had to pull me into an extraordinarily hot shower to stabilize me. These only happen when the subject of spirits comes up and I am particularly exhausted.

It doesn't even matter if I am intellectually aware that everything is OK or not – the panic attack is involuntary. If my parents had been sensible and sought out a doctor for me at the beginning, none of this would have ever happened.

I would not have shut out my peers during those vital years and would probably have cultivated more stable friendships as an adult. Panic attacks, general anxiety and depression would probably not have developed as I entered adulthood.

My father is no longer with us, but I have not told my mother that it was actually sleep paralysis that troubled me all of those years and of the incredible harm that she has caused. I think that enough harm has been done by her ignorance and that nothing can come out of pointing out that gigantic shortcoming other than launching her into a depression herself. That is, if she believed me to begin with.

Quite frankly, more than enough people are on pills in this family as it is.